Wildlife

WILDLIFE
MIRANDA BEESON

Poems

Spuyten Duyvil, New York City

Contents

One

CUTCHOGUE, APRIL 1, 41.0107° N, 72.4851° W

The fish hawk is back, surveying his nest from his usual perch
—an edifice of twigs, twisted sea grass, popped rainbow
birthday balloons, a red shred of t-shirt, the glitter of tinfoil
from picnics on the beach—the detritus of man.

Soon his mate will arrive from the tip of a peninsula
in French Guiana, squeezing the Earth's magnetic field
for signs pointing north over the Caribbean, to Hispaniola,
Cuba, riding the thermals sixteen hundred miles home.

Somewhere on the Aegean between Turkey and Greece,
citizens are squeezed together in zodiacs that know nothing
of stars. They huddle under the weight of water-logged
life jackets and fear—a tiny motor sputtering its way

toward unfamiliar lights over a sea of broken paddles,
backpacks, glittering lost cities.

CONTINUOUS PRESENT

With the slice of a knife a man in yellow waders
guts his fish. It's a big catch. Striped bass.
The boats have just come in. The docks
are slick with iridescence and death.

We are spending a Sunday afternoon in Montauk,
watching the water crows in Ditch Plains,
walking the town, eating grilled cheese
sandwiches in the light blue retro coffee shop.

Julianne Moore strolls by, charisma with kids.
I think about the film *The Hours*, how Julianne's
character, suffocating in the skin of the American
Dream, flees—*I chose life*.

On the drive home I remember a dream
I had years ago. It took place here on the bluffs,
although I knew I'd never been here before
(an uneasy déjà vu). A skin-deep party,

late summer, a woman's insinuating dress.
In reverie and reality I begin to wonder—
What's next? Out beyond the shore, far from
docks, a silver fin cuts the surface of water.

THE KILLERS

The wife asks if you would like a drink—even though the house belongs to friends of yours. Her effortless dress & edgy tattoos skim across the familiar floor.

She opens a cabinet, poses a glass in her tapered fingers, pours you a small pour from a dark bottle of red, extends the glass less than halfway exacting servility.

She rests her hand lightly on the wing of her etched husband as he grazes by, suited, man-bearded, a crisp of linen & money.

You ask if they live nearby by way of saying nothing. *Oh yes.* Her Oh the flicker of other residences. Her taut arm, sword of silk, cuts the air between you & the bay.

You watch her red painted toes curl up, then settle back down into the inviolable security of her strappy heels.

Down behind that little white sign we're always told is too hard to find. Well—way down behind. His family's place. She compasses the room for her husband.

Their eyes meet. Transaction complete. *What are you writing about?* she inquires, gazing away. You, you think to yourself. I am writing about you.

ALPHA BOARS

Radioactive Boars in Fukushima Thwart Residents' Plans to Return Home

We light our wild boar way through deserted streets. A dim burn
at dusk, our tusks bright as Jupiter by midnight.

The fungi at the fungi farm turned bright blue. They were the first
to radiate. I crave shiitakes—we snuffled them all up.

Those first few years were glorious. No 2-hooves in sight. Rats
took supermarkets. All-night parties in the soba noodle aisle.

Dogs kenneled 2-hoove dens, tore down doors, looted cupboards,
curled up on down-filled quilts. Off-leash at last.

Yes, we finished off some chicks, but I-me-mine hotfooted it,
leaving their hens & cows & hogs in pens to starve & die.

We were more humane. I say every beast should live in clover
& die a quick, good death. We are but links in great food chain.

My piglets gleam. Born neon-pink, they grow saber tooth tiger
tusks, rippling mercury fur.

My little tribe runs wild, tusking here & there. No fear. I had
forgotten too, but 6-year news came—x 2 are doubling back.

Shots in the night. News of culling, furnaces, mass boar graves.
Brutal 2-hooves on the move, but not for long—

for we are nuclear-boar-strong now. We have shining x-ray eyes.
Our hooves flick atomic fire.

SUNRISE HIGHWAY BLUES

After the princess
—the Nassau County kind
Mercedes GLA Coupe—
said *I wasn't texting*
meaning she was
when she totaled
my Mazda Hatchback
you were driving
because you were too
cheap to buy new tires
for your old truck—
After her daddy pulled up
phone to phone
bristling & brilliantined
in his Porsche Cayenne
SUV & cursed you out
because she was a
daddy's girl—
After I picked you up
outside the ugly ER
where you sat cross-legged
on a patch of lawn
smoking a long
brown cigar—
I curse you out for
becoming the man
you always were—
You've got no sorries
no please baby please
I'll pay you back—
just the pay-back
a man lays on a
woman when
he's no longer the
center of her universe—
You say—
You're a bitch like
all the rest of them
I say—
Yeah baby, but
not your bitch.

Two

ROCK, PAPER, SCISSORS

Carol's just back from Chappaquiddick where they sell jars of oil
    for drowning ticks at the corner store. A local boy showed her
        where the Kopechne girl died. She thought it would be a mansion
            by a lake, but it was just an old shack by a brackish pond.
                The boy said Mary Jo was pregnant, I say Rose made
                    him do it like Mother at the Bates Motel.

When I was little my brother and I had different ways of killing a tick,
    all of them horrible. Sometimes we'd skit it back and forth, using two
        wood matches for sticks, crouched on the warm tar road in front
            of the hedge, back from the beach, salty and bored.
                Then we would set it on fire.

I would tell myself later in my prim twin bed, under the dark roar
    of August's cicadas that my brother made me do it, but knew
        it wasn't true. Knew the stock-still second of orange ignition
        made my skin prick alive.

REVERSE DRIVE

after Nate Marshall

Your blue VW reverses from a tree it hits in Mattituck. You are 25. You come back to life, back up east on the stormy north road to the Shelter Island ferry that churns a reverse spume to the other side, back up the last hill on the island to our house, where the stairs lead back down from your room to the driveway where your two-seat Karmann Ghia is parked, first car, (first girl), first neatly rolled joint tucked into the tiny glove compartment next to the cassette player jamming B.B. King's Lucille, while an LP is spinning music out the window of the house, (me, your sister, Beatles backward), reverse down the drive in our parents' not yet battered-by-years Country Squire station wagon to the DMV where you ace your test because you pass it before you take it, leaving your bike down by the bay, where you row the dinghy back out to the daysailer you sail to Connecticut to pick me up, where I am dancing a dancer's reversed life in front of mirrors the summer of my 16th year, our English Bulldog slobbers his way back to us, we are learning to sail on our little red twelve footer, I am crew not captain because I am your little sister following your blond nod through tall snow banks on Riverside Drive NYC to the #5 bus that drinks exhaust down to 79th, dropping you off, me cross-towning, but don't have to as I am already in class, we unlearn everything from 12 to K, dreaming of life without homework, our uniforms becoming looser then smaller, our book bags lighter and lighter, our spoons in our grabby hands at the red kitchen table, the chrome high chair, the stove with four legs, two naked babies in a steel wash tub in the tumbling green yard of the farm house (that will become a farm) on the island where our mother is wearing blue overalls, looking up at us from a head of lettuce she is about to pick from her garden, just sprouted, a seed in the ground, a packet in her hand in the hardware store with a drawing of a lettuce under the word Burpee, a mid-winter wish in her mind for next spring while she watches us sleep, hopes she can have children, meets our father, wonders about love.

INLAID

a marquetry box 5 x 7 persian from the land of rumi & rhyming couplets
    [before nukes fundamentalists & oil]
mother-of-pearl from the great green turban snail & ivory
    [before everyone began to think about where everything came from]
tortoise shell from the hawksbill sea turtle
    an endangered species inlay set like old fashioned type
[when sentences were metal letters made into words on a composing stick]
    box and sycamore   [when trees belonged to themselves]
rosewood like a song   perfumed interior   [the passage of time]
    stubby yellow pencil from days of board games points & ice cream
pink pearl eraser   [when pencils were pencils   erasers erasers]
    six silver paper clips   three brittle red rubber bands
green sea glass   [when sea glass could still be found]
    two shells   [a scallop & a cherrystone]
my mother's box of odds & ends & dreams
    there's a barge parked outside my window on the hudson tonight
[a long rectangular shadow on the surface of the river]

THE SCORPION'S TAIL

Two Scorpios in a car, my 3rd driving instructor Bill says as we navigate the road
I must learn to drive which happens to be the road my brother died on.
I say your name.

Saw the date on your driver's license, Bill says, letting me know he knows my age,
adding the word anal as a Scorpio descriptor while I make a tight right on to
the road I swore I'd never drive.

Tried the highway. Too fast and furious, I tell Bill. I lie & know I lie. I feared
the speed—the need to be right next to you. Christopher.

Slow down. What does the sign say? Bill asks, super-placid. 30 I reply. I am doing
50 trying to stick it to the grave. (I drive under the spell of ptsd.)

Pivot, Bill says. Pivot what? I reply. Your heel, Bill says. I cannot pivot. I will never
be 9 & 3. Good with rear view mirror & blind spot, Bill perks up, unfamiliar
with metaphor.

Our father once told me from the deck of the house they bought after you died,
Your mother asked me to say—please don't drive the car. I say your name.

LADY SPEED STICK

years ago at the beginning of the twenty years
        i spent wanting to be
        someone other
        than myself
i would stand in the long cool aisles of pharmacies
        and pick a certain brand of antiperspirant
        lady speed stick
        light musk
i would buy the one with the apricot top
        because i wanted
        to smell like
        a certain girl
a girl who was dating a friend of mine
        we shared
        a beach shack
        way back when
she was one of many girls i wanted to be like
        blonde
        blue-eyed
        sleek as a fast car
nothing seemed to stick to her from
        sand to sadness
she wore a different bathing suit
        every blunt
        shiny day
the summer my brother was killed in a car crash
        light musk was one
        small choice
i could make in the stunned aftermath
a choice to smell like that girl who left my friend
        for a man with a
        bigger bank account
she was heartless but i could not think
        of anything
        i wanted to be
        more than that

A NESSUNA COSA

The wild-eyed Chinese man who came to pick up the carpets,
paced them off, one shoe per foot, muttering in Mandarin
until he saw your piano.

Piano, Piano, Piano he shouted, racing across the Persians,
opening the lid, sitting down, hands poised momentarily
in the air, before pouncing on Mozart, con brio.

Then he closed the lid as quickly as he had opened it,
rolled up the carpets, heaved them over his shoulders
and dashed out the door.

His fermata remained, echoing across the high
white ceilings, the walls where the paintings used
to hang, the burnished bare floors.

KAREN'S DELI

The long fluorescents bless the tops of the heads of those who wait
in the a.m. for bacon egg & cheese on a roll that'll be three twenty-four.

Salt-Peppa-Ketchup? Deb's sacrament requires a simple nod or not
in reply, right down the line, always a next, never a last, although

sometimes it's ham. Phyllis' diamond slides to the side when she rags
the counter, Nicole's is newer & smaller, & Ethel's chin is red again

for the third time this week. So much sex, so much happiness. So many
eggs cracked, scrambled, fried, wax-papered, brown-paper-bagged

born on the griddle of God's grease, while the *Post* remains stacked
high & well-thumbed by those who wait. No purchase necessary.

Two napkins per from the chrome container to the left of the register
which still dings (not a celestial ring) to celebrate the arrival of cash

(no credit). Another nod & a dollar tucked into the small rectangle
cut out of the lid of a plastic quart container. We say grace.

Three

FOR LOVE OF AN ORANGE

With the reduced
use of organophosphate
& carbamate
insecticides
katydids have
become
more numerous.
If you detect
leaf feeding
it is time
to apply an
insecticide.
If diflubenzuron
(Micromite)
or cryolite
are planned
apply before petal
fall because
they are
slow-acting.
Micromite
does not kill
the katydid
until it tries
to molt.
Cryolite
is a stomach
poison that
slowly kills
the katydid
over several
days. Katydids
can cause a lot
of damage
in a short
amount of time,
so killing
them quickly
is important.

We are singing
in our long row
of orange grove
this evening.
Green on green:
we are leaves
& leaves are we.
Our nightly
syncopation:
wing to wing
scraper & file—
chirp, click,
swish, buzz,
rattle & trill.
Many duets.
Petal fall—
supped our fill
& an aphid
or two.
One satiation
leads to need
for another.
Like you—we
are made of
brain & heart
ganglia & gland
trachea & tube
ova & sperm.
The males bring
nuptial gifts.
Our antennae
touch & smell
one another—
male to female.
Like you—we
mount & thrust.
Live to live.

THE LEXICON OF TWO

Your blonde loft on Franklin Street before Tribeca became Tribeca.
You behind the lens, me in front—wanting to bypass the laissez-faire.

We were made for *molecular knitting*. Couscous the cat watched (or not)
as we *consumed* each other on the pickled floor. We were made to be
each other's *skin particulates*.

Where was that dirty little cafe with those round tables too small for
any kind of two? MacDougal Street? Or was it Bleecker? Where you
steeled yourself against me. I would return the favor, years later.
Then you, again. We were made for *volatile activity*.

Up top Malibu, above Point Dume, you'd take Betty the old Land Rover
down with your board—Quica and Juno riding shotgun Australian-
Shepherd-style through the chill California morning.

The dogs *milling & pressing* the surfers on the beach.

We'd hike the scrubby hills, the dogs running ahead, then *catalyze*
each other one more time. You were painting the Fractal Ellipses.
Living on brown rice & red wine from admirers. Finally *decanting*
yourself just right—& you knew it.

You were my *pressure tank*. Always telling me to write.
What are you writing? Write. Mine the *substrate*.
Find the *fine soft mud*.

Was it LAX where we *evaporated* one more time? Racking our povs
into two decades of me vs. you, you vs. me—*cell* by *cell*?

The *oxidation* of time.

That hotel in Santa Monica with its low sheered bed. The Bougainvillea
bursting just outside the terraced door. Remember? After the exhibition
of your work? The one you hoped & waited for?

We lay clothed beside each other, your lungs struggling to expel CO_2.
We both knew you were *fermenting* death. We held hands, talked about
your cool new Vans, our lives, & art—words we poured into each other,
made of love.

PANTHERA PARDUS

No need to behave like a badly trained hit man
shooting randomly at elusive targets after a
late night out—you're home. It's merely me.

Or to reenact the Battle of Bull Run when it's
merely CVS calling to say your prescriptions are
ready. It might be a good idea to pick them up

and adjust your amygdala. It's just the sapiens
mind missing its fishtail days in the warm swamp,
the snaky, green jungle we used to call home—

when fight or flight was a daily carnivorous event.

These days we're both upright mammals with vestigial
paws that won't get us far should, let's say, a leopard—
in all her tawny glory—appear on the lawn.

But what are the chances of that?

We're homo sapiens (wise), with hare triggers
screaming (did you hear the death rattle
of that rabbit last night?)   Leopard—

when it was merely a series of inconsequential
spots in the dark—stars, planets, fireflies,
embers reflected in my green eyes.

FOR THE EX OF YOUR CHOICE

You were a sheep, a wolf, a charmer, and a bastard.
Cock of the walk, well-combed too, you beautiful bastard.

Praise for others before me, and after, and those kids,
well, the _____ one was like you, a crazy bastard.

Still stuck up there on the cross of your _____ childhood?
My God. You had it (and us) all, you lucky bastard.

Chameleon-like, you lizarded your way into hearts
that swooned for you, and I bet some still do, poor bastards.

No longer silent—to hell with our Miranda rights,
we hereby ghazal you—you cheeky, yes—rat bastard.

At the winery on Friday night, you switch tables to join a male friend as the evening waxes & wanes. Heads turn. Female heads. Women who are sitting at the table deciding you are younger & more fuckable. You're probably not younger, but yes, more fuckable. It's a state of being not an organ. Just give me the edge on the end you say to your friend. He makes room for you in the middle instead. It's one of those worn picnic tables we know from childhood. The ones with happy memories. Or not. You could squinch in, but these days you're feeling feral so you straddle the bench. So wife's away guess this is the mistress? one of the women quips. The other women yip. You miss the next line, but there is one. More yips. The women should know better, but are no better than old-coyotes-can't-get-it-up-no-more at a bar. They snuffle the hot air. Detect you are not a member of their pack. You are a packless alpha. You like it like that. Your upper lip retracts. You slide your pink tongue over your white fangs. The moon is up as you circle in for muscle, sinew, viscera.

Four

THE STONE'S ALIVE WITH WHAT'S INVISIBLE

after Seamus Heaney

Orange core of heat
    blue crush of ice
        concentric ring of tree
            flat land of serengeti
                ambered beetle dung
                    claw of triceratops
                glacial lake jagged peak
            bone of man feral dog
        first fire scrub of ash
      blade of grass chip of axe
drop of blood

ARIA

At twilight we watch small dinosaurs
stalk the waters of the salt meadow.
They are herons, but the slant of light,
the time of day coinciding with the end of the season
makes the mind press against the inevitable
desiring something ancient and immutable.
Salty and shoeless from our swims,
feet on faded brick still warm from the sun
...the first shadows have begun
to sift down around us.
First it is the Great Blue Heron
with his patient prehistoric stride,
followed by Maria Callas, the Snowy Egret,
then the lesser Egrets: a mailing of trim white letters.
Is this how change announces itself?
Birds become dinosaurs, and opera singers
are followed by letters from abroad
announcing the time has arrived
to reinvent the world all over again.

NORTH FORK BARN BLUES

When we were a farm, I had three tall stalls. One for the old gray
mare. Remember that tune? One for the work horse. Milk cow too.
Up where it was warm? My hay loft—sharp, stickety & sweet.

When roads were dirt & dung, when young boys went to war
& never came back. Fields fold over time. Now it's bikes, kites
& pseudo-canoes. The bronze monuments? Long gone green.

Train tracks shined pearl from oyster shells spilling from barrel
after barrel headed west to the red brick mansions of the rich
before the beds of men & shellfish were laid bare by income

tax & greed. One in the same name. And you thought *my* name
was nostalgia? That's a man's word for a world that never was.
The one a man wished for, but never got around to living

before he was gone. Dust to dust, ashes to ashes my right-now
owners sigh as they bury their little black dog right behind
my unoiled door. Back where the aspen tree weeps.

Why do they make their dinner outdoors? That's what a woman's
kitchen is for. They worship the god of charcoal in its metal grate
forsaking the uprightness that is pew & praise on Sunday.

A sin not to know to whom & what to pray for. Dinner won't get
you nowhere near heaven. And from where I stand, this current
crop is quick-stepping straight down to that red hot location.

Hollering & flickering late-night-lights on small devil screens.
What ever happened to chair, book & two-for-two pleasure in bed?
Don't sing *she ain't what she used to be* to me. I've seen it all.

Plainer then. Tawdrier now. Three wars, full forty families here
& gone. All that's tall, silent & green chopped up for fast food
& cold music. I'm still here, two hundred years & counting.

Five

CATCH & RELEASE

The old man unzips the zipper
of his cakey pants, the toddler
in his stroller investigates his
snot, a countertenor (earbudded)
croons to what could be Bach
up above the screech & roar
of ungreased wheels, the #1 train
streaks into Lincoln Center, exit
singer, enter schizophrenic
explicating x-rays & salt shakers
while Pale Lady across the way
adds eyebrows to her face—she
a queen, we her courtiers—we
stare & decide to turn away.

He stares as you decide to cross
the pack of poets on the con-
ference lawn. His eyes say fuck
in the best sense of that word.
And so, the royal poet, all irony
& wit, writes himself right into
you. With each new (rosé) wine,
imagined groins align. Shazam!
Glances slam across the storied
lawn. A hit of fire power at last.
Let's put this sex to use: set lit
match upon a page (or 2), fire
up the engine of desire, catalogue
the wild hawk-eyed heart.

Stormy Daniels hawks her
heart for 130 K / or maybe
#manypublisherscompete?
D T: #hazardsofthejob, #u-
electedme & #calculated risk.
S D: #intothelionsden, #high-
wireact, #gotatigerbythetail.
#devilinabluedress? Monica
Lewinsky—#weremberu.
Retweet: #iftheglovedontfit
acquit, #itsajungleoutthere,

& #flirtingwithdisaster...
magnet to magnate? I say—
Stormy D: ready aim fire.

Fire, magma & lava—the
Great Dying—252 million
years ago & all due to CO_2.
Let's think on this as we
gas up our Odyssey minivans
for epic trips to drop off kids
in schools that spell danger
with a D for dual-purpose
weapons, deputies on patrol,
deterrent options, dispersion,
& diazepam under a cloud of
halocarbons. No Vesuvian
hiss this time, but home-grown
killers: we are the volcano now

that we no longer choose to
remember. *We have The Magic
Flute!* the dementia gang hollers,
this they can remember—
the residents of the Memory
Palace (kings & queens of
über NYC) are fed up with
Mozart & his shenanigans.
*Bring us some ballet, bring
us The Wizard of—* ?
Where is their Emerald City?
Why are their brains made
of straw? 3 clicks & you bring
new DVDs. Your mother beams.

And how about your family?
beams the perfectly nice lady
at the luncheon under the din
of ladies of certain age. Pale
cubes of what a woman
should be nestle on the cheese
plate next to the Triscuits.
You go for option #1: *28
cousins scattered all over
Europe.* Very la-di-dah.
You pass on #2 & the 3Ds

the alliterated one you love:
death-divorce-dementia.
It's a luncheon after all.

Nice cleavage a woman
remarks from the mat
next to yours at the gym
while you are holding plank.
10-9-8-7-6-5-4-3-2-1. You're
not sure it's a compliment.
You say *They're all yours!*
realizing tits are the last bit
of a woman men can't stop
staring at. Later on one of
the retired dicks at Karen's
Deli puts his hands on you
while saying *Could you
push it in a bit? Your chair?*

The moon stares across a
country road—silence falls
on the lawns of the rich. The
long field down the way strip-
ped of sod again. Bared brown
3 times this long summer. A
bright emerald cut & pasted
carpet for the mansion to
to the East. The owner roars
Hedge not straight enough!
Dark-skinned men scurry to
4 square its green. Mowers
mow, blowers roar & blare.
Quiet. Winter does not care.

*Haven't seen that old raccoon
around* (not that you care)—
*the one big as a camel who
humps across the lawn at dusk.*
Yr. neighbor raises one eyebrow
signifying what he's done &
defends—*I saw him peering
at me through the fence.*
(Looking = capital offense?)
In these parts it's police pistol
to raccoon head. A wildlife

control guy once clued you
in: *Catch & Release? Where?*
They're better off dead.

The star-nosed mole can
catch his prey faster than
the eye can follow. A tiny
twenty-two pink-fingered
snout with 100,000 nerve
fibers fires off mini-me-
messages to mini-mole
brain. What's not to love?
Worm! Worm! Worm!
Worm gone—¼ of second.
Size of a finger tip & yes—
blind. Mini-mole navigates
his world by snout in his
snug black tunneled dugout.

Donner Party takes short
cut in 1847 under the spell
of manifest destiny. Expansion
is our right! Tunneled under
20 feet of snow, they starve.
Rescue Party Letter Home:
Children found sitting upon
a log, their faces stained with
blood, devouring the half-
roasted liver and heart of their
father. Eliza Donner, survivor:
Remember never take no cut-
offs, and hurry along as fast
as you can.

Do you have kids? the
overheated mother asks
after you pay too much
attention to her two who
are reading sweaty library
books on an August afternoon.
Her Q is not a Q. It's—I still
make eggs—don't see none
in your coop. Don't snoop
in mine. I rule the roost.
No rooster jokes come to

mind so you say to her kids—
Oh! The Wizard of Oz!
I loved that book too.

The lawn guy says *You*
look good... Long winter.
No mowing. You stacked limbs.
No need for him. Now—
another cold spring. Cut
your hair off, completed
a degree: the pleasures
of being female without
a male ...*like Barbie!* he
completes his compliment.
Tiny head—no brain,
you reply, leaving him to
wonder why that matters.
Exit tits.

All that could have been
yours, your well-married
friend sighs. The tycoon
who wanted to take you
to Paris, well—*take* you—
fell off his stallion under
the influence of Chivas
(not lying) dying young-
ish. Coulda Shoulda?
But you only loved his farm—
& cows, soft beauties—
each with her name et-
ched on her elegant stall—
waiting to be milked.

In my studio, I'm happy
as a cow in her stall.
That's the only place
where everything is all
right. Provocateur of
black matte seductions,
Louise Nevelson
created sky cathedrals
from cast off scraps.
At her retrospective?
I've been here all the

time darling, you just
weren't looking. (She lived
in the 4th dimension.)

How old are you? the
very nice retired gent
queries over G&Ts
on the lawn by the bay
in front of their aging
house. By way of saying
why aren't you like my
wife? I don't understand
your life. *I'm as old as you'd*
like me to be, you reply.
It is not a satisfactory
answer, but you let it sit
there anyway. *Good*
clamming today?

Ex Chief of Staff in
Bob Woodward tell-all:
When you put a snake
and a rat and a falcon
and a rabbit and shark
and a seal in a zoo
without walls, things
start getting nasty
and bloody. Solution:
Snake eats rat. Falcon
eats rabbit. Seal calls in
team to take on shark.
Humans live on in alt-
media amusement park.

In this blazing summer
of wildfires & melted roads,
England's emerald fields
thatch brown—in cropmarks
—the dead reappear. Roman
settlements, animal pens,
henges & fossilized trees.
The word EIRE burned into
the side of a hill in WWII:
to flying aces racing the sky,
dizzy from delivering death—

Don't bomb here. You are home.
The natural world scorched
by the hand of man.

Six

DEVIL #1

Lucifer lay your red hot pointy ear next to tiny pink mine
Let me feel the claw of your crow-taloned hand
Oh! The long lithe length of your thigh
Sling your arrow-tipped tail. Snap it my benighted way
Ensnare me. Tangle me in your untangled heart
Peal me open. Mine my hubris. Excavate my conceit
Brand me with pride. Ride me into the prize of thee

THE GUNSLINGER'S TALE

Let's say that in somebody's world
all the guns were taken away
just hypothetically.
We still have cars.
We still have white vans
like in Toronto.
We still have other means
of people committing
mass carnage.
So eliminating any guns
doesn't help.
I have good friends
who I don't see
eye to eye with.
People can hopefully
come to a common
ground.
What we can't come
to a common
ground
with
is people on
the other side
that say
we want to
take *this* gun
today
because
they'll always want
to come back
and take *that* gun
tomorrow.
The best we can do is
mitigate the carnage.

THERE'S A RATTLE, SOMETIMES

after Gwendolyn Brooks

Are you lost? Where is your home? My morning address to the
ants who are marshaling the kitchen counter. A strange earth
for this staggered colony of desperate valiant specks. There is
no there, here. Directionless, they scatter, regroup & lay down a
wobbly trail across the white expanse of stove in one beautiful
act of determination after another: sheer persistence to find a place
to nest, a crevice between faucet & formica. Watermirrors
their ant selves, sink spray is rain falling on dry antennae &
oases appear here & there under a just washed coffee cup. Things
so ordinary to we large ones are porcelain palaces & pools to
you who carry bits of toast like Atlas shouldering the world. Be
gone! I plead as I watch this morning's news. A woman reflected
in steel, pierced by rebar, falling from a border wall. Goldenrod
(she can see it through the links) blooms in San Ysidro USA across
the way. She has traveled in a word made for pilgrims & traders: the
Muslim caravans from Cairo to Damascus, the Silk Road bearing little
pots of spices, honey, gems, paper & slaves across desert & lagoon.

ODE TO A DIME

July 4—for Brae

You keep appearing, shiny & sincere, everywhere I go.
First I forget to zip you into the pocket of my wallet where you live.
So you fall out—into my hand.
I stuff you back in with the big paper bills.
(I was rushing—sorry.)
Next I find you by the brake pedal of my car.
How did you get there?
I pick you up. Stop the day. Look.
Oh Dime! You are so much finer than fat quarter,
clunky nickel & the usual slew of dim pennies that
tag along behind.
Slimmer—
your edges fine serrated pleasure—
you are the clearest of clear thoughts on a cloudless day.
Your roundness? Minute, yet exquisitely complete—
& you are always bright.
Why have I never *seen* you before?
Now I find you on the table by the screen door
where those artless car keys relax.
And so it goes.
I learn to leave you where I find you.
Contemplate what lies behind face value.
Friends come to visit—you are on the bathroom floor.
They place you on the counter by the sink.
How intimate. Oh Dime!
—you have been humidified.
That dime, I say, has followed me around all week.
Their son says you are made of magic.
He balances you very patiently on a door knob.
Knob? Faux gold. You? So—silver. (You like this...)
And so—I palm you.
Study what you carry with you everywhere you go—
Lit Torch & Olive Branch—
Tall Oak & FDR
& 3 small words.
E Pluribus Unum.
Out of many—one.

THE TRAD-WIFE'S TALE

I always wanted children that looked like me:
     blond-haired, blue-eyed babies, but kind of had
          to say it under my breath.

My great-grandfather came looking for land
     during that great immigration period. There
          was an abundance of property in the Dakotas.

I spent the last decade of my life living overseas.
     I started to see a marked increase in peoples of
          North African descent, women wearing burkas,

young Turkish mobs attacking Germans, unwilling
     to learn their language still wanting to gain from
          their system. An influx of refugees took over

the country. I came home.

I always felt bad that I was attractive. I was
     ashamed I was a white North American blonde,
          blue-eyed female. I tried to fit in, be more spicy,

listen to more diversified music, tan my skin darker.
     I have never been happier or more fulfilled as I am
          now with my heterosexual white husband.

And I have to say, everyone—I don't care if they're
     Hispanic, Black, Mulatto, Indian, Native American,
          everyone has said they have never seen such intensity,

such beautiful blue eyes as we have on our child.
     And I think, you know what? That's right.
          We did that on purpose.

Manolo me Mammon
     You gold-encrusted god of plenty
Park me on Park Avenue
     Gild my walls. Chandelier my halls
Jet my days. Jaguar my bluestone nights
     Pool me in my private Mediterranean
Yacht me & unstopper me
     Margaux & Coach me
Cover me in coin. Booty & Botox me
     Multiply my capacity for rapacity
Artichoke roast & spit me
     Braise & flambé me
Let me live in your insatiable need

THE TYRANT'S TALE

A Bill of Indictment

Let facts be submitted to a candid world.

He has refused his Assent to Laws, the most wholesome and necessary
for the public good.

He has called together legislative bodies for the sole purpose of fatiguing
them into compliance with his measures.

He has erected a multitude of New Offices, and sent hither swarms of Officers
to harass our people,

and eat out their substance.

He has kept among us, in times of peace, Standing Armies.

He has combined with others to subject us to a jurisdiction foreign to our
constitution:

For cutting off our Trade with all parts of the world. For taking away
our Charters, abolishing our most valuable laws, and altering fundamentally
the Forms of our Governments.

He has excited domestic insurrections amongst us.

We have Petitioned for Redress in the most humble terms:

Our repeated Petitions have been answered only by repeated injury.

A Prince whose character is thus marked by every act which may define a Tyrant,
is unfit to be the ruler of a free people.

THE JAVA SALOON

Yup. He's always tyin' me up—& not like with his go-to-girl.
I'm a woofer, canis lupus familiaris to you & yup, I watch.
Sometimes they do it woof way but with no tail it's a no-class
act. You can see his dawg bobs fly up & down. Good his bitch can't.
If my bitch saw mine she'd scram outta town. And they think
tails are for wagging. No man—they're for class during the act.

So I'm tied up like horse to hitching post & he's off to the Buck
Star—ain't no old fashioned saloon (old dude's all tricked out).
Buck's all about Grande, Venti, Trenti. Just like La Lupa first
She-Wolf. Gave tit to Romulus & Remus. (Spoke Latin too.)
One wanted one hill, the other, another. Bro sicced Bro.
One lives. Other dies. Homo Sap—got no respect for pack. OK—

he's back, slurping & yapping on his Sap-Device. We woofs dig
our chow in a bowl by the back door. With luck? Leftover chop.
Yup, he cut mine off. Thinks I should take it lyin' down like
his bitch & yup my snout tells me she's doing more than just his.
We know. They don't. Other way around? I'd snap him to a leash
in a skimpy frock. Heel bitch. No Buck Star for you. SIT.

SMOKING GUN

A curtain drawn
over a torn star,

we divide, nurse
grudge & conquer

our long divisions.

Empty crowds
simmer in light

dimmed by fools,
educated by rule—

a Johnny-
come-lately.

We hymn sweet
our dead weddings

& sorrow—graves
shallow & deep,

buried under a
calm weight

of easy listening—

of credit sold
& days bought.

We curse, supply
demand & swear.

A false mess of
hot hope.

DEVIL #3

leviathan sea monster   mount of anti-christ   twisted coiled & supreme
call me   la créme de la créme   jewel in your crown   desire of all desires
teach me to   crave & hanker   hunker me down   in pilfered eiderdown
call me the envy   of every gal in town   inspire me to covet   wish & crave
lead me to live   in each & everyone   of your synonyms   carve me emerald
polish me green   call me by your name

Seven

Asmodeus wrathful & divine
Three-headed bull-ram-man
Tail of snake
Mouth of flame
Born of king & succubus
Lance me with your lust
Ride your serpent-headed dragon
North between my east & west
Master & slave
Shackle & flame me
Iron my wine
Pulp my juice
Lavish me like Luxuria
Lost in covetous desire
Make me crave
Hanker & pant
Seventh prince of hell
Make me an arrow
In your lascivious quiver
Devour & demolish me

XX/XY

after Lila & Lenù

first blood flows
you think
it's a cut
not realizing it's
the unkindest cut of all
you can bear
children now
you are an
ungrown
grown up
you are 12
years old
ducking into
unknown toilets
to unpin & pin
tape & untape
blackened blood
its mild stench
you know
everyone knows
the bus driver
the no-longer
kid friends
(the pre-12
pervert who
no longer
proffers his
penis to you
in the park)
teachers & traitors
on the dry periphery
far from your
wet white thigh
freezy december
hot red leak
you are a freak

you live on a
clotted planet
of pink slips
& butch gym
teachers: *may*
i be executed?
(a freudian slip)
you hatch it out
excused?
it's my aunt flo
i'm on the rag
red flag
crimson tide
(not) mother
nature's gift
(not) red badge
of courage
but shark week
i am cursed
1st tampon
your mother
outside your
13-year-old b/r
push it in
you say
which hole?
bloody & terrified
blue school uniform
peter pan collar
shorted knee socks
lace-up oxfords
i only have 2 holes
where's the 3rd?
where should
i push it in?

knowing as you
find the 3rd
it's all over
the climbing tree
the kid to kid
pat & walk the dog
being as alive
& unseen as
any creature
can be before
i take u / mate u
from now on it's all
guys & power
what he's got
& what you got
breasts legs & curls
girls against girls
you got yours
& you learn how
to use it & re-use it
you are flirted
unshirted still
not knowing
the why of it
you learn to give
it & take it
x-ing your xx's
for his xy's
first blood
flows

HERE IS SELF'S JUNGLE AJAR

Humbert is all of us

we craved you
black sheep son of a gun
millionaire
waiting for us every day
after the 310 bell
with nothing but
time on your hands
slim-hipped at Starks
sueded
unsocked
soft maid-washed-shirt
tails out
tousled
we craved your
ice cold gifts
you'd say
it's called gelato
we'd say *we know*
pistachio all around
you cruised us
we cruised you
my marble foyered girls
birthed by alabaster
raised by hired hands

all appetite & ache
we craved your
low-slung jaguar
first cruise control
the yes & no of it
must have both &
all at once please
we played cock tease
laid bets down
hung on the funk &
power & glory of it
ride around the park?
why not? so what
if your dick came
along for the ride
his tan hand
on your bare knee
hot breeze cool heat
we were in the arena now
call it greed & need
the knives are sweating
in the drawer

PROPOSALS

From my theater teacher
Who ran his right hand
Quick & hard
Between my legs
Clit to hole
Right before my entrance
On stage
Off Broadway
Go be my girl!
From my gynecologist
Who always pressed
His fat, fleshy pelvis
Up against
My naked shoulder
Right by my mouth
As I lay splayed
Clamped & cold
On his examining table
I want you to be fulfilled.
From my therapist
Who popped the question
Mid-session
Instead of
Saving my life
I love you
Put your hand
On my dick
Will you marry me?

MOTHER OF ALL BOMBS AKA MOAB

It was a hard labor.
He arrived pointy
and hard, weighing
20,000 pounds,
30 feet long, packing
11 tons of TNT.
Compared to my
little guys—the 250s,
he was a doozy.
So big I had to
deliver him
out of the back
of a cargo plane
on a pallet with
the help of a
parachute.
Sailed straight
down into caves
and tunnels
where soldiers
for the other
side hide—the
Afghan mountains
that enfold
field upon field
of bright red
poppies. A
blooming
afterbirth.

A taut woman takes the seat next to yours on the jitney to nervy NYC from countryside by sea. Her gloves were all the rage a few decades ago. You know—the felt-like ones you'd get for Christmas when you really wanted red kid—before you knew what "kid" meant. Black with gray racing stripes. Velcro closures. It's July. Germaphobe? You make a note. She's twitching the twitch of I must have my way with the world. She surveys the size of the bag perched on your knees. It's large, like your life. Large & Full. You keep reading Carlo Ravello, Ch. 6 "The World is Made of Events, Not Things," while charging your iPhone & listening to Glenn Gould having his way with Bach. You are wired every which way into your world, and she'll be having none of that. You wait for it. Felt-like tap on your shoulder. You refuse to unplug. Another tap. You unplug one earful of cantata. *Would you like me to put that bag up?* she states, pointing to the it of it. *Thank you. I'm fine*, is your measured reply. She shifts in her seat, stunned at your refusal to inhabit her reality. Ravello is writing, "The entire evolution of science would suggest that the best grammar for thinking about the world is that of change, not permanence. Not of being, but of becoming."

Eight

A DEPARTURE QUESTIONS DARKNESS

breaking distant & early
a thing with no name
(caesura'd)
a distant sorrow
a distant darkness
(caesura'd)
we doze   nulled by lullabies
a wick   extinguished
no words for   (caesura'd)
individual — self
a void of scattered   certainties
an indefinite   article
we trickle   quilted refrains
(caesura'd)
upside-downing
icy phragmites
fire — earth — water
(the "a" of air)
breaking   distance
a flesh — a mind
(caesura'd)
dulling nulling
day upon day
a purification
a retreat
(caesura'd)
we seek
respite
to begin
again
to
"a"

COUP DE FOUDRE

Did you lose your keys? I say
Rolling down my car window
On a wild windy mid-June day
By the bay. White caps, the bridge
& you. Talk about cinematic.
Why do you look just like John
Slattery in Mad Men? All cropped
White hair & vigor? Can I say—
You are life force made flesh?
Your stunned expression stuns
Me right back. A woman drives
By & rectifies the wreckage of
Your day. What are the odds?
(Your black credit card too...)
I say *I knew it was you*, not
Knowing why, but knowing
I knew. The magnetic field of
Feeling—the absence of thought.
I found them washed up on
The beach. Down there. Where
I live. Follow me. And you do.
A strange intimacy—watching
Happiness fracture the face of
A man you just met. Its naked
Beauty. I hand you your keys
& card—keys worn & warm,
Card sleek & hard. We are palm
To palm. Pull me through the
Words of the world where words
Matter. Sever the slice of late
Afternoon sun that falls between
Us. Let me slip out of my skin.
Slip into yours.

THE JONES OF IT

For a time it cut through conversation, car metal & spare parts.
It pierced glass, split spinnakers, reversed propellers, roiled the bay,
sheared sand.

It rose tarry & thick off paved parking lots, shot through the slots
of my shopping cart, sucked AC out of the frozen food aisle,
pooled ice cream, wilted green beans.

It juiced watermelons, spitting flesh & seeds high as July fireworks.
Algae bloomed hot fluorescent, fish jumped six feet high, rods
cast a mile out into the bay.

Dogs panted not knowing the why of it, the cat (skittish & wild) lazed
out long on the hot deck. Screech owls screeched midday. Mourning
doves moved on.

Potted plants drooped & whined. Cold water ran hot. Planets flamed out.
Night laid down a new trail. You knew if you put your hands on me—
it would burn.

The shimmer & shackle of it.

Nine

THE SMITH'S TALE

In the low shadowed corner
of my mid-winter 3 a.m. room
stands a sad hulk of a man
hump-shouldered & silent,

his stiff sooty clothes
layered like shingles on
the house of his soul. The
blacksmith's apprentice—

his molten days flowing
one through the next in
a succession of horse shoes
& hitching posts, hammers

& tongs. A solitary spirit who
has refused to leave this 18th
c. smithy, currently the house
of my 21st century friends.

I have had such visitations
before. Fright does not factor
in, only a palpable curiosity—
why a weight won't lift.

You have seen it, I'm sure.
The last fierce struggle
followed by an ascension
—the relief in the room—

a body turning the color
of clay, the eyes dim pools—
but such a lift, shift in the air—
like a longed-for breeze.

He regards me, hooded brow,
black eyes, this neanderthal,
all spite and sorrow—a plea
for help made flesh.

Blacksmith, heal thyself,
I say. I am busy carrying
my own weights, measuring
out my own molten days.

Either hammer the iron
or lie flat on the anvil, waiting
to be struck. Smite those
chains—link by link.

HOME DEPOT

Surveying sample kitchens
with Lila
we turn past oak & granite
to find José
her co-worker, clutching
his cell phone
sobbing.
My favorite uncle in Mexico
just died—died &
no money for airfare.
José's raw grief
leaning on a kitchen counter
that will never
provide food or comfort
is heartbreaking.
You cannot remain unmoved
in its presence
although Lila does.
She is Chinese with
gold cat eyeglasses.
We are only here temporarily
Lila says—
directing my attention
to a simpler kitchen
by Martha Stewart.
What about this one?

ODETTE/ODILE

Exiting the dementia ward locked/key-coded, never-arriving elevator, you decide to turn towards, not away from the screaming woman in a nearby room.

Her voice a harsh loud rasp, her words foul & desperate as a sailor's in a violent storm. She is continually drowning, never drowned.

You take her mesh-gloved hand in yours calibrating her ability to accept kindness. You know the quick dark flash,

how quickly she can unleash what we keep under lock & key: our cornered beast.

You know the gloves keep her from tearing at herself, just as you know your mother will rub her eyes not knowing she is blinding herself.

A ballet dancer, her aide tells you. Danced all over the world. Neck of swan, high fair brow, hair pulled back, grace of arm & leg still here.

You look into her wilding eye, tell her she is beautiful. She bows her head like dancers do at each & every curtain call.

QUICK NOW, HERE, NOW, ALWAYS—

for my mother

Think of it as a long slow bank & descent,
a plane curling light as air through cumulus.
The slide & jive of jetting through ice crystals.
(They say that's what clouds are made of.)
There, there's the Earth as seen from up above,
a bright mosaic giving way from time to time
to glittering clusters of cities
& water, always water.
Its embrace of land so clear from up here,
how one fits hand in glove with the other.
(Remember how we used to swim & swim?)
Swaths of houses sit trim & undistressed.
Byways course like veins through the body
of the country, a cantata of light & speed.
Vehicles the size of childhood toys zip along
shining paths towards their destinations.
The living world moving in unison... complete.
I say this to you. Look! Look down.
It is so beautiful. You have lived here.
It is waiting for you. Land.

JACOB'S LADDER

I am taut. I am light. I am fair. He who made me was the same. I am a thing of turned posts. I am slatted, ladder-backed, milled by the circular saw of my creator. My finials are clear-stained, temperate, self-sufficient. Purity rests in my pine and in those who take their rest upon me when the day is done. They rest in the knowledge all things are in their place. And I have found my place among them.

I am neither man nor woman, and long to be neither. I know nothing of strife, covetousness, wrath, vice. A soldier shall never take his rest upon me. From time to time when they dance, shake, quake in what some call ecstasy, I think on other ecstasies than simplicity. I know, but I also know better. I remain celibate and celebrate God in my uprightness.

I am grateful I have never wanted to be anything else but what I am. Do not consider me placid, but prudent, peaceable—happy as I am. A ladder-back chair made by a man who followed the words of a woman named Ann who experienced a divine light. I am that light too.

Ten

TERN PIERCING WATER

How can it see its prey
From so far up?
Dive so fast?
Accomplish so much
—so quickly?

Feral cat beheads
Mouse on deck
Head left wedged
Between wood
Eyes wide open.

I'd love to talk but
I need to get a glass
Of water. She turns
On her heel to attend
To herself.

Lolliguncula brevis
An unexpected approach
Strike & recoil—also
Known by the name
Brief Squid.

Red fire licks
Green hose. Black
Boot heel. Matted pine
Needles ignite
Tinderbox.

Trigger finger
Jacketed lead
Propulsion
Empty chamber
Soft flesh.

Three crows chasing
A white owl: 6 a.m.
A swoop behind
Trees. Black on
White in flight.

Lunch? Yes please!
Your guests say
Turning to leave
For the beach
Head of lettuce.

We don't do mice
The wildlife guy says
Handing you two
Peanut butter
Baited traps.

It's going to rain
She tells you the day
Before your beach
Party. She stares
You turn away.

On the upper deck
On a damp night
A slight disturbance
In the air. Scything
Nearby.

Irises push out
Of dung & yard
Discards. Green
Chemise. Dark
Blue eyes.

WHAT I REMEMBER FROM MY TIME ON EARTH

I remember many first days of school. And that empty feeling.
I remember, after eating ice cream too fast, a cold head rush.

Children playing
jacks in street
make a play of shades
make a play of lights.

I remember magic carpets and giant genies, and trying to figure
out what my three wishes would be.

I open the first door.
It is a large sunlit room.
A heavy car passes outside
and makes the china quiver.

I remember wild red poppies in Italy.

     * * *

It's true, we did that earlier, but this time
I want it slow. He's undressing,
telling me about the new, humane circus—
no tigers or bears.

My tongue moved, a swung relaxing hinge.
I said to him, What will become of us?
And as forgotten water in a well might shake
At an explosion under morning

Or a crack run up a gable,
He began to speak.
I remember searching for something you know is there, but it isn't.

* * *

I open door number two
Friends! You drank some darkness
and became visible.

Between my finger and my thumb
The squat pen rests; snug as a gun.

IN YOUR DREAMS

Truth be told, I am not very accommodating.
Have you seen my tail? The crest on my head?
My eye? Brilliant as a black diamond?

Darwin thought he sighted me as he labored
through endless guano on that rocky island.
But I eluded him, as I have many others.

Some say they have seen me above the tall
masts of ships as they prayed to the heavens
during violent storms.

Others say I am a species of heron, last seen
in South America—with eelgrass caught
in my tail. How prosaic.

Rorschach determined I was an ink blot,
Jung, an archetype, even Freud chimed in
—something to do with hysteria & women.

I know you find my tail disturbing. Don't.
It was a gift from a small girl in Denmark.
One very long lock of her hair.

She was the one who understood I live in
your imagination—real as anything unreal
can be. Or unreal as what you call—real.

SPEAK/LISTEN

Because their leaves look like angels' wings,
I say—naming this summer's begonias.

Their blooms? Orange like splitting open
melon, no deeper. Like fire, well, cooler.
Like carrot, no hotter. Say, devil-orange.
Orange like you hope orange could be,
the way you hope heaven will be (if
there is one) when you get there.

Speaking of wings, it's a Sunday afternoon.
The wind came up at one after a still morning.
Still as flat rock with turtle, flat as horizon
line—but the Earth's spinning isn't it?
You say still like napping cat, closed green
eye, flicking tail at play with sun.

The tall oaks (they have seen it all) speak.
Long branches meet air in great swaths of
motion. A whoosh, then another—leaves
punctuate long sentences of maple. A rustle,
no quiver, like thick brush on canvas, owl-
wing, heavy feather, light touch.

What is the word? No matter, no matter.
We are listening, listening—

DARK PALETTE

Untitled, 1955, Mark Rothko, Pace Gallery

Green of green
  four-squared forest
    of light
      enter

Blue of blue
  smooth release
    into water
      dive

Slate of slate
  sky stretched and held
    by your hand
      stay

Plum of plum
  day's end in free fall
    time
      unspooling

Rust of rust
  familiar scar on a body
    made of love
      touch

Black of black
  sits in her habit
    chanting
      stand

Color of color
  encircles the untitled
    world
      begin

Notes

"Continuous Present" references Gertrude Stein's phrase in "Composition As Explanation," published in 1926 by Leonard and Virginia Woolf's Hogarth Press.

"Reverse Drive" is after the Nate Marshall's poem "Palindome," which is after Lisel Mueller's poem "Palindrome."

"A Nessuna Cosa" references a musical notation to hold a fermata until it dies away.

"For Love of an Orange" excerpts text from the website of University of California's Agriculture & Natural Resources Integrated Pest Management Program.

"The Lexicon of Two" utilizes language from the lexicon for the fermentation of cider and wine.

"Catch & Release" sources ideas and text snippets from the following *New York Times* articles: "The 8 Million Species We Don't Know," Edward O. Wilson, March 3, 2018; "When Life on Earth Was Nearly Extinguished," Peter Brannen, July 29, 2017; "A Road Map of 'Crazytown'," Dwight Garner's book review of *Fear: Trump in the White House* by Bob Woodward, September 6, 2018; "The Mysterious Landscapes of Heat-Scorched Britain," Paul M. M. Cooper, August 15, 2018.

"The Gunslinger's Tale" excerpts verbatim text from the transcript of an audio interview, "National Rifle Association Member Discusses President Trump's Speech at Meeting," May 4, 2018, *All Things Considered*, NPR.

"There's a Rattle, Sometimes" is a golden shovel from the first stanza of "The Third Sermon on The Warpland," by Gwendolyn Brooks. The title is drawn from the second stanza of same.

"The Trad-Wife's Tale" excerpts verbatim text as transcribed from an audio interview: "How the Migrant Invasion Made me a Trad Wife," Radio 3Fourteen, April 23, 2017, originally sourced from "The Housewives of White Supremacy," Annie Kelly, the *New York Times*, June 1, 2018.

"The Tyrant's Tale" is excerpted from part three of the Declaration of Independence.

"XX/XY" is after the novel *My Brilliant Friend*, by Elena Ferrante.

"Mother of all Bombs aka MOAB" references the GBU-43/B Massive Ordinance Air Blast, commonly known as MOAB, "Mother of all Bombs." It was first dropped on April 13, 2017 as part of a US airstrike against the Islamic State targeting ISIS tunnels in the Achin District of Afghanistan.

"Quick Now, Here, Now, Always—" is a line from T.S. Eliot's *Four Quartets*.

"What I Remember from My Time on Earth" is a cento from the poems of Joe Brainard, Luis Garcia, Seamus Heaney, Tomas Tranströmer & Patricia Young.

"In Your Dreams" is an ekphrastic poem inspired by the Mixed Media Collage, "Accommodation" by Nadira Vlaun.

Acknowledgments

Thank you to the following journals and their editors for the initial publication of versions of these poems:

Badlands "Cutchogue, April 1, 41.0107° N, 72.4851° W"
Barrow Street "Coup de Foudre," "The Smith's Tale"
Bateau "Rock, Paper, Scissors"
New Millennium Writings "Home Depot," "Ode To a Dime,"
    "The Lexicon of Two"
Palette Poetry "There's a Rattle, Sometimes"
Pedestal Magazine "XX/XY"
Shrinking Violet Press "A Nessuna Cosa," "Aria"
The Best American Poetry "Devil #2"
The Laurel Review "Alpha Boars"
The Southampton Review "North Fork Blues," "Reverse Drive,"
    "Karen's Deli"
Typishly "The Jones Of It"

Gratitude to many who were instrumental in the writing of these poems and the creation of the manuscript itself. In particular: Matt Coonan, Caroline DeLuca, Natalie De Paz, Anthony DiPietro, Lauren Francescone, James Hytner, Tyler Allen Penny, Claudia Acevedo-Quiñones, and Zinnia Smith. Gratitude to mentors and readers: Cornelius Eady, Lynn Emanuel, Julie Sheehan, and Terese Svoboda. Gratitude to my best longtime reader, Paula Shengold. Gratitude to my students, who write fine poems and inspire me to do the same.

Special thanks to Molly Peacock for being the poetry mentor of a lifetime, to Michael Gregory Stephens, and to Tod Thilleman, Editor/Publisher at Spuyten Duyvil.

Spuyten Duyvil
© 2023 Miranda Beeson

Book Design: Lauren Francescone

Proofreader: James Hytner

Author Photograph: Caroline Knopf

Typeset in Arnhem and Weiss

Library of Congress Cataloging-in-Publication Data

Names: Beeson, Miranda, author.
Title: Wildlife / Miranda Beeson.
Description: New York City : Spuyten Duyvil, [2023]
Identifiers: LCCN 2022053650 | ISBN 9781956005950 (paperback)
Subjects: LCGFT: Poetry.
Classification: LCC PS3602.E36677 W55 2022 | DDC 811/.6--dc23/eng/20230215
LC record available at https://lccn.loc.gov/2022053650